Contents

Introduction

'If it can be proved that I have an honest right to my income, I am just as ready as any other person to enjoy it. But if it cannot be proved, I will give up my position here. I cannot suffer all this pain.'

For nearly ten years, Septimus Harding has been the warden of the hospital for old men at Barchester. It is a well-paid job, although there isn't very much to do. The men have a comfortable home, good meals and some money – and they are happy. But suddenly the Church and its ways are under attack. Young John Bold begins to look closely at the warden's job and believes that Harding should be paid less and the old men more. A powerful national newspaper joins the attack on the Church. Harding would love to resign but his masters won't let him. Can this bitter argument somehow be settled?

Anthony Trollope was born in 1815 in London. His family was poor because of his father's failure in business. Trollope worked for the post office and rose to a high position. He was sent to Ireland in 1841 and wrote his first novel there. But his first real success was *The Warden* (1855), based on a real case concerning the Hospital of St Cross, near Winchester. This was the first of six 'Barsetshire' novels, set in a cathedral town in the southwest of England. These novels are still very popular, especially *Barchester Towers* (1857). Trollope was a very energetic writer and produced over sixty books. Forty-seven of these are novels. He died in 1882.

The Warden

ANTHONY TROLLOPE

Level 5

Retold by J. Y. K. Kerr
Series Editors: Andy Hopkins and Jocelyn Potter

Pearson Education Limited
Edinburgh Gate, Harlow,
Essex CM20 2JE, England
and Associated Companies throughout the world.

ISBN 0 582 41818 6

The Warden first published in 1855
This adaptation first published by Penguin Books 1995
Published by Addison Wesley Longman Limited and Penguin Books Ltd. 1998
New edition first published 1999

Second impression 2000

Text copyright © J. Y. K. Kerr 1995
Illustrations copyright © Kay Dixey 1995
All rights reserved

Typeset by RefineCatch Limited, Bungay, Suffolk
Set in 11/14pt Monotype Bembo
Printed in Spain by Mateu-Cromo, S.A. Pinto (Madrid)

Published by Pearson Education Limited in association with
Penguin Books Ltd., both companies being subsidiaries of Pearson Plc

For a complete list of the titles available in the Penguin Readers series please write to your local
Pearson Education office or to: Marketing Department, Penguin Longman Publishing,
5 Bentinck Street, London W1M 5RN.

Chapter 1 Hiram's Hospital

A few years ago there was a clergyman★ called Septimus Harding, who lived in the quiet cathedral town of Barchester, in the west of England. Barchester is more famous for its beautiful cathedral and various fine old buildings than as a commercial centre; and its most important citizens are considered to be the bishop★ and the other clergymen of the cathedral, together with their wives and daughters.

Mr Harding had come to Barchester early in life. He had a fine singing-voice and a deep love of church music. For many years he remained an unimportant member of the cathedral staff, where his work was light but not well paid. At the age of forty he was put in charge of a small church close to the town, which increased both his work and his income, and at the age of fifty he was appointed precentor★ of the cathedral.

Mr Harding had married young and was the father of two daughters. The elder, Susan, was born soon after his marriage; the younger, Eleanor, not till ten years later. At the time when this story begins, Mr Harding was already the precentor at Barchester and was living with his younger daughter, having been a widower for many years. His elder daughter had married the bishop's son just before her father's appointment, and unkind tongues in Barchester whispered that his daughter's good looks had got him his job as precentor; but in this they were probably wrong. The fact remains that Susan Harding had married Dr Theophilus Grantly, the son of the bishop, archdeacon★ of

★ A clergyman is any church official. In the Church of England the head of a cathedral is a bishop, who lives in the bishop's palace. His senior manager is the archdeacon. The precentor is responsible for music at the cathedral services.

Barchester and the clergyman responsible for the church at Plumstead Episcopi, a village outside the town.

There are unusual circumstances connected with the position of the precentor which must be explained. In the year 1434 a rich man called John Hiram died, having made his money as a buyer and seller of wool. In his will he left his house and some of his lands near the town as a charity for the support of twelve old men. His will said that these men must be people who had lived all their lives in Barchester and who had worked in the wool business before old age and ill health forced them to retire. John Hiram also ordered the building of a hospital, or old people's home, for the twelve to live in, and, beside it, a house suitable for a warden for the hospital, who would also receive annually a certain amount of money from the rents of Hiram's land. Finally the will said that the position of warden should be filled by the cathedral precentor, if the bishop agreed to the appointment.

Ever since that time this arrangement had continued. The wool industry no longer existed in the town, so the bishop, the archdeacon and the warden took turns in choosing suitable old men – old workmen who were grateful to receive a comfortable home and one shilling* and fourpence a day, the amount fixed by John Hiram's will. About fifty years earlier they had received only sixpence a day as well as their meals, but, by general agreement, the change to a daily figure of one shilling and fourpence a day was made.

This then was the situation at the time when Mr Harding became warden, and the old men thought themselves lucky to be so well fed and looked after. But the situation of the warden himself was even more fortunate. The lands once owned by Hiram had greatly increased in value over the centuries and were

* A shilling is twelve old pence or a twentieth part of a pound.

now covered with houses. A gentleman called Mr Chadwick was employed as the manager of Hiram's land and buildings, and the money received in rents from these was paid to the warden. After making the daily payments to the twelve old men and giving them their meals, the warden was left with an income of eight hundred pounds a year, not including the value of his house; by contrast, his position as precentor brought him only eighty pounds annually. Some people did sometimes whisper that John Hiram's money was not fairly divided, and such whispers had come to Mr Harding's ears; but being a fair-minded, generous man, and feeling that there might be some truth in these observations, he had decided to give each man another twopence a day, paying this amount from his own pocket. He explained to the men that this extra money was a gift from himself and that future wardens would not perhaps continue it; but the men expressed themselves quite satisfied with the new arrangement. Mr Harding's generous decision, however, did not please everyone: Mr Chadwick, for example, considered it to be unwise, and the warden's strong-minded son-in-law, the arch-deacon (the one person whom Mr Harding was really rather afraid of), was violently against it. But the warden had already informed the men at the hospital about the increase, so it was too late for the archdeacon to interfere.

Hiram's Hospital, as the place is generally known, is a pleasant old building which stands on the bank of a little river that runs near the cathedral. Beside it sits the handsome old house of the warden, with a pretty garden round it, and here Mr Harding lived at the age of nearly sixty, his hair beginning to turn grey, dressed always in black, with his glasses on his nose or in his hand. He was not exactly a hard-working person, although he had written a book about old church music, which was his greatest love. He had greatly improved the singing in Barchester cathedral, which was now as good

3

as any in England; and his strong voice led the church services. More than anything he loved to play the cello – with or without an audience. Mr Harding did have one weakness, however: he had no head for money matters. He was generous to all and especially to the twelve old men in his care; yet he lived in continual fear of Archdeacon Theophilus Grantly, his son-in-law, who watched over his finances with the greatest attention.

Mr Harding had been precentor at Barchester for ten years when rumours about Hiram's Hospital and its finances began again, as part of a movement by various people in different parts of the country to criticize the Church of England. Mr Harding himself had no guilty feelings either about his work as warden or about the eight hundred pounds he received for it, but two of the old men in the hospital were beginning to say that, if old John Hiram's will was carried out properly, they would each be enjoying a hundred pounds a year. One of this discontented pair was called Abel Handy, a man to whom the warden himself had given the first vacant place that appeared at the hospital.

Also living in Barchester at that time was a young man called John Bold, who did much to encourage the dissatisfaction expressed by some of the old men. He and Mr Harding knew each other well and could even be called old friends, in spite of the difference in their ages. Dr Grantly, on the other hand, considered John Bold a trouble-maker and thought of him as his enemy.

John Bold's father had been a successful doctor in London. When he died he left most of his money to his son, who had just finished his medical studies. John, who was then only twenty-four years old, decided to set up house in Barchester with his unmarried sister Mary and to begin work as a doctor in the town. Barchester, however, already had nine other doctors, and after three years Bold found that he still had very few patients. He was a clever, rather daring young man. Having enough money to live on, he interested himself in putting right all sorts of social injustices. He defended the poor against the rich, the weak against the strong. He was quick to act and sure of the rightness of his actions, as any well-educated, self-confident young man can be.

Dr Grantly observed Bold's actions with alarm and thought him a dangerous rebel, but Mr Harding remembered how young Johnny had come to his garden as a child and listened to him playing his cello, and he could not bring himself to dislike him. In fact he was not the only person in his family who took an interest in the young doctor. His daughter Eleanor disliked hearing John criticized by others, though she dared not defend him to her brother-in-law. She encouraged her father to continue receiving Bold, in spite of his political views. She was unwilling to go to houses where she would not meet him and, in a word, she was in love. Nor was there any good reason why Eleanor Harding should not love John Bold, since he had all those qualities likely to touch a girl's heart. He was brave, enthusiastic and amusing, well-made and good-looking, young and active. His character was excellent. He had a large enough income to support a wife; he was her father's friend; and, most important of all, he was in love with her.

Dr Grantly was quick to notice the way the wind was blowing and was not at all happy about it. He had not yet spoken to his father-in-law on the subject because he knew that the warden's love for his daughter was so great that he could not refuse her anything; but he brought the matter up in private with his dear wife, as they lay in bed together in their bedroom at Plumstead Episcopi. Dr Grantly was a gentleman of impressive appearance and the highest principles.

In public he was a greatly respected figure: his forceful manner and strongly held opinions created fear, even terror, in the hearts of the people of Barchester. It was only when he took off his shining black clergyman's clothes and put on his nightshirt that he began to talk, look and think like an ordinary man.

'My dear,' he said, gathering his nightshirt around him, 'that John Bold was at your father's house again today. I must say that your father is most unwise to receive him.'

'He has never been very wise,' replied Mrs Grantly from her comfortable position under the blankets. 'There's nothing new in that.'

'No, my dear, I admit that. But at the present time his foolishness is − is − I'll tell you this, my dear: if he's not very careful, young John Bold will be off with Eleanor.'

'I think he will too, whether papa is careful or whether he isn't; and why not?'

'Why not!' almost screamed the archdeacon, 'why not! That bad-mannered, interfering adventurer − the least respectful young person I've ever met! Do you know that he's putting his nose in your father the warden's business in a completely unacceptable, most − ' Unable to find words strong enough to express his feelings, he finished his sentence with 'Good heavens!', spoken in a manner which always caused a great impression at church meetings.

'I cannot agree with you, archdeacon, that he is badly behaved. I certainly don't like Mr Bold; I think he is much too pleased with himself. But if Eleanor likes him, and they decide to get married, that would be the best possible thing for papa. Bold will never cause trouble over Hiram's Hospital if he's papa's son-in-law.' And the lady then turned over in bed in a way which showed that she had no wish to discuss the subject any further that night.

Dr Grantly was not a bad man. He was quite intelligent enough for the work he had to do. He carried out his duties at Plumstead Episcopi faithfully, but it was as archdeacon that he really shone. In most cases where there is both a bishop and an archdeacon, one does all the work and the other does very little. In the case of Barchester, the worker was the archdeacon. He was confident, a good speaker, quick to make decisions and firmly fixed in his opinions. Above all, he was always determined to defend the interests of the Church from outside attack with everything in his power.

As for Mr Harding, he saw no reason why his daughter should not love John Bold. He had noticed her tenderness for him, and his main regret over the action which Bold was about to take concerning the hospital was that this might separate him from his daughter, or else separate her from the man she loved. He was certainly not going to turn his back on the man his daughter loved just because he held opinions which were different from his own.

Until now Bold had not taken any action concerning the hospital, but he had heard of the complaints made by some of the old men there. He had also heard that the income from Hiram's land and buildings was very large. He decided therefore to call upon the manager, Mr Chadwick, and ask for information about how the whole organization was financed. He soon discovered that, if he interfered with Mr Chadwick as the manager, he must also interfere with Mr Harding as the warden. This situation was regrettable, but he was not a man who could allow personal considerations to decide his actions.

Having now become interested in the matter, he began to examine it with his usual energy. He got a copy of John Hiram's will and studied the wording with great care. He found information about the houses built on Hiram's lands

7

and their value, and worked out how the income from them was divided up. With this information he called one day on Mr Chadwick and asked for details of the income and of the amounts of money spent on the hospital over the last twenty-five years. Mr Chadwick naturally refused the request and said that he did not have permission to make these facts public.

'And who is able to give this permission?' asked Bold.

Mr Chadwick informed him that he must turn to the hospital's lawyers, Messrs Cox and Cummins of Lincoln's Inn. Mr Bold wrote down the address, said the weather was cold for the time of year and wished him good morning. Chadwick agreed about the weather and showed him to the door.

Bold went immediately to his own lawyer, Mr Finney. Finney advised him to write to Cox and Cummins at once, demanding a complete history of the hospital's finances.

'Should I not see Mr Harding first?' suggested Bold.

'Yes, yes, of course,' agreed Finney. 'Mr Harding is not a man with experience of business matters, but I don't think that seeing him can do any harm.' Mr Finney could see from the expression on John Bold's face that he intended to do things his own way.

Chapter 2   A Shadow of Doubt

Bold at once set off to the hospital. He knew that Eleanor usually went for a drive at this time, so he would probably find Mr Harding alone. It was a pleasant June evening. The little gate to the warden's garden stood open and, as Bold went in, he could hear the sweet sound of Mr Harding's cello. The warden was sitting on a garden chair, playing some of the much-loved church music he had collected in his book. Around him sat, lay or stood ten of the twelve old men who lived under the hospital roof. The two rebels were not there. Recently they had kept away from the warden, whose music was no longer to their taste.

One of the listeners was Mr Bunce, a big handsome figure of a man, although he was over eighty. Bunce was the unofficial leader of the twelve and made no secret of his loyal and affectionate feelings for Mr Harding. The warden was equally fond of Bunce and would often ask him in to drink a glass or two of wine with him on cold winter evenings. Bunce now sat listening and looking at the warden admiringly, as he played his heavenly music.

When he saw Bold walking towards him the warden immediately stopped playing and began to make him welcome.

'Please, Mr Harding, don't let me interrupt you,' said Bold. 'You know how fond I am of church music.'

Mr Harding had been expecting a pleasant social chat and he looked rather puzzled and displeased when Bold told him that he had come to discuss business matters. 'I wish to speak to you about the hospital,' said Bold, 'and most particularly about the hospital finances.'

'My dear friend, I can tell you nothing. I am like a child in such matters. I only know that I am paid eight hundred pounds a year. Go and talk to Chadwick; he knows all about the financial situation. But tell me now, how is Mary Jones with her bad leg?'

'She's improving. But Mr Harding, I hope you won't be displeased by listening to what I have to say about the hospital.'

Mr Harding gave a deep sigh. He was very much displeased at the idea of discussing this subject with John Bold, but,

9

not knowing how to avoid it, he sighed again and said nothing.

'I have the greatest respect for you, Mr Harding, and I do not want you to think that what I'm going to do comes from any personal dislike on my part . . .'

'Personal dislike! That's unthinkable!'

'I believe that the Church is not properly carrying out John Hiram's will and I wish to examine the matter.'

'Very well, I have no reason to refuse you, if that is what you want; and now we need not say another word about it.'

'Just one word more, warden. Chadwick has given me the names of your lawyers and I consider it my duty to ask them for details of the hospital finances. If this seems to you to be interference, I hope you will forgive me.'

'Mr Bold,' said the other, 'if you act fairly, speak nothing but the truth and do not try to deceive us in carrying out your purpose, I shall have nothing to forgive. I suppose you think that I do not deserve the income which I receive from the hospital and that this money should be given to others. Believe me, I shall never think badly of you just because you hold an opinion different from my own. Do what you believe to be your duty. But here comes Eleanor with her horses, so let us go in and have tea.'

Bold, however, felt uncomfortable at the idea of sitting down with Mr Harding and his daughter after such a conversation and so he excused himself with embarrassed apologies. He simply lifted his hat to Eleanor in greeting as he passed her, leaving her surprised and disappointed by his departure.

Mr Harding's calm manner impressed Bold, making him think that the warden was sure of his position and that he was about to interfere in the private matters of a fair-minded and respectable man. But Mr Harding himself was far from satisfied with his own view of the case. Could it possibly be that John

'I believe that the Church is not properly carrying out John Hiram's will and I wish to examine the matter.'

Bold was right and that for the past ten years the warden had been receiving an income that legally belonged to others? For the first time in his quiet, happy, respectable life a shadow of doubt fell across his mind and for many, many days to come our good warden was neither happy nor free of self-accusing thoughts.

Eleanor noticed that her father seemed unusually worried as he sat drinking his tea, but she was more concerned about John's sudden, unfriendly departure. She supposed that there had been some kind of quarrel between the two men and felt half angry with both of them, without being able to say why.

Mr Harding thought long and deeply, both before going to bed and afterwards, as he lay awake questioning the rights and wrongs of the income he enjoyed. Was John Hiram's will being fairly carried out? That was the real question. He knew how strongly Dr Grantly would support his position, but he did not want Dr Grantly's support. He decided instead to admit his doubts and share his thoughts with his old friend the bishop; and to the bishop he went, the morning after John Bold's unwelcome visit.

The bishop, now over seventy, was the very opposite of his son the archdeacon: not active and forceful but gentle and kind. The bishop and Mr Harding loved each other dearly. They had grown old together and over the years they had passed many hours considering the business of the Church in all its details. Now that their children had married and Mr Harding had become precentor and warden, they were all in all to each other.

Up to this time the bishop had heard nothing of the trouble at the hospital, so it was a long explanation which Mr Harding had to give before he could make the bishop understand his own view of the matter. At first the bishop's solution was to refer the whole problem to his son. 'No one understands the matter so well as the archdeacon.'

'But, bishop,' said the warden, 'did you ever read John Hiram's will?'

The bishop thought he might have done, about thirty-five years ago, but was not completely sure of the fact.

'But, bishop, the question is, who has the power to decide these things? If, as the young man says, the will demands that the income from Hiram's lands should be divided into more equal shares, who has the power to change it?'

The bishop thought that such changes could take place with the passing of time. He said something about tradition, and spoke of the proper difference between the needs of a clergyman in Mr Harding's position and those of a number of poor old men supported by the Church. He laid his hand on Mr Harding's knee and Mr Harding understood that he felt sympathetic towards his old friend in trouble. And this, thought Mr Harding, was the reward he had come for.

There was a silence for a little and then the bishop asked almost angrily whether this 'trouble-maker' (John Bold) had any friends in Barchester. Mr Harding had already decided to tell the bishop everything – to speak of his daughter's love as well as his own troubles – and now was the time to do so.

'Mr Bold is much liked in my family, bishop. Indeed, I like him very much myself. It is not impossible that he will one day be my son-in-law.'

The bishop's amazement was plain to see. He almost whistled aloud but, being a bishop, did not.

'I don't mean they are about to be married, just that they are very fond of each other,' said Mr Harding hurriedly.

'But, Harding, how can you stand against him if he is to be your son-in-law?'

'But I am not against him; it is he who is taking sides against me. If my position has to be defended, I suppose Chadwick will do it.'

13

'Oh, the archdeacon will see to that. The archdeacon will never allow family relationships to stand in the way of doing what he feels to be right.'

Mr Harding made the bishop promise to say nothing of Eleanor's love for John Bold, especially not to the archdeacon; and then he said goodbye, leaving his poor old friend feeling both amazed and puzzled.

◆

The case of Hiram's Hospital and its income, which was about to cause such a storm in Barchester, was slow to reach the twelve old men themselves; but Finney the lawyer had been mixing with them, helping to increase their dissatisfaction and feeding their hopes of getting rich. In fact the old men's important needs were already met: good food, clothes, a well-heated home and plenty of rest after the hard lives they had led; and a kind, true friend to look after them if they were ill or unhappy. John Bold himself sometimes had doubts about whether the old people's lives would really improve if they got one hundred pounds a year instead of one shilling and sixpence a day; but he quickly buried such thoughts.

'Each one of you ought by law to receive one hundred pounds a year' was the message which Mr Finney whispered in Abel Handy's ear. Handy was not slow to tell the other eleven and to win support. Mr Bunce, of course, could not be persuaded to change sides and with him two others remained loyal to the warden. Of the other men, five supported Handy and three were undecided. Mr Finney had prepared a petition which listed their wrongs and requested justice for their case, promising to send copies to all the important newspapers in London; but so far only six of the men had signed and this would not make a good impression. The undecided ones were Job Skulpit, Billy Gazy and Jonathan Crumple.

'Well, Job,' said Handy, 'you're ready to sign, I think. Here's the place, do you see?' and he pointed to the dirty piece of paper in front of them.

'Just think, Billy Gazy,' said another of Handy's supporters, 'a hundred a year and all to spend! Just think of that, old Billy!'

But Billy's only words were, 'I don't know. I just don't know.'

'Come on, Skulpit,' said Handy. 'You're not going to be like Bunce and let that old churchman rob us all. Take up the pen and ask for what is yours.'

'But then,' said Skulpit, apologizing for the delay in his signing, 'our Mr Harding's not so bad. He did give us twopence a day, didn't he now?'

'Twopence a day!' cried the others.

'Twopence a day!' shouted Handy. 'You want me to go hat in hand and thank the man for twopence a day when he owes me a hundred pounds a year? No, thank you!'

And so the old men argued this way and that until Gazy, Crumple and finally Job Skulpit were persuaded to put their marks on the page, since none of them could write.

'Well, now all nine of us are in the same boat,' said Handy, 'and old Bunce and his friends can – '

'Well, Handy, and what can old Bunce do?' The upright figure of Bunce himself appeared in the doorway.
'You've been doing no good here, Abel Handy, that's easy to see.'

'I keep to my own business, Mr Bunce,' said the other, 'and you should do the same. Your spying on us won't do any good either.'

'I suppose then, Job,' Bunce continued, 'you've put your name on their paper at last.' Skulpit looked ready to die of shame. 'I've known you, Job, since the day you were born,' said Bunce, 'and I tell you now you've done a foolish, wrong thing. You've turned your back on a man who's your best friend. You're playing the game of these others, who care nothing for him, whether he's rich or poor, well or ill, alive or dead. A hundred a year? Are the lot of you so soft in the head that you think you're all going to get it? Aren't you getting everything you hoped for, and more than you hoped for, already, when before you were too poor and weak to earn your daily bread?'

'We want what Hiram left us. We want what's ours by law.'

'Law!' said Bunce bitterly. 'Did you ever know a poor man made better by law or a lawyer? Will Mr Finney ever be as good to you, Job, as Mr Harding has been? Will he visit you when you're sick and offer you sympathy when you're depressed?'

'No, nor give you a glass of wine on cold winter nights. He won't do that, will he?' cried Abel Handy and, laughing at his own cleverness, he and his colleagues left the room victorious, carrying with them the now powerful piece of paper.

Chapter 3   Dr Grantly and the Petitioners

Though doubt and uncertainty gave our poor warden a sleepless night, his brave son-in-law suffered from no such weakness. Dr Grantly was fully confident of the rightness of his case. His greatest aim in life was to defend the interests of the Church against any kind of attack from its enemies. Such work demanded courage and energy, and the archdeacon certainly had plenty of both.

A day or two had passed since the signing of the petition. 'Well, Mr Chadwick,' he said, walking into the hospital manager's office, 'anything from Cox and Cummins this morning?'

Mr Chadwick handed him a letter, which the archdeacon read with great attention. Messrs Cox and Cummins simply reported that no word had yet been received from the opposite party and suggested that it would be wise to approach Sir Abraham Haphazard, the attorney-general.★

'I quite agree with them,' said Dr Grantly, giving back the letter. 'Haphazard is without a doubt the best man for the case. Of course we must have him.'

Having settled this point to his satisfaction, he walked over to the hospital to learn how matters were going there. The archdeacon, for all his good qualities, was not a man especially alert to other people's feelings and, after greeting the warden in his sitting-room, he did not hesitate to deliver an attack on the 'unspeakable' John Bold in front of Miss Harding, though he rightly guessed that the lady had a certain fondness for his enemy. Eleanor still knew nothing about Bold and the crisis over the hospital, but she sensed that things were somehow going wrong.

'We must do something – and soon,' said the archdeacon firmly. 'Of course you have heard of the petition?'

Mr Harding admitted rather unwillingly that he had heard of it.

'Well?' The archdeacon waited for Mr Harding to express an opinion, but none came. 'We can't allow these people to get an advantage over us while we simply sit and watch them.'

The warden continued to look at him in silence, while his

★ The attorney-general is the senior legal adviser to the government.

fingers made the movements of someone playing the cello – a sure sign that he was upset.

'Cox and Cummins say that we must employ Sir Abraham Haphazard for this case, and I quite agree with them,' went on the archdeacon.

The warden's fingers played a slow, sad tune. He thought uncomfortably of his income being examined, his modest life, his daily habits, his undemanding work.

'I suppose they've sent this petition to my father,' said Dr Grantly.

'I really don't know,' answered Mr Harding.

'What I can't understand is why you let them do it, when you are in charge of the place and have Bunce to help you.'

'Do what?' asked the warden.

'Why, let young Bold and his awful lawyer Finney prepare this petition. Why didn't you tell Bunce to destroy it?'

'That would hardly have been wise,' said the warden.

'It would have been very wise, if they had done it among themselves. I must go to the bishop's palace and answer it now, I suppose; and a very short answer it will be.'

'But why shouldn't they send a petition, archdeacon?'

'Why shouldn't they?' said the archdeacon impatiently, at the top of his voice. 'I'll let them know why they shouldn't! I want to say a few words to them all together.'

To the warden this idea was most unwelcome, because privately he had decided not to interfere in any action the men might take in the matter. He strongly wished neither to accuse them nor to defend himself. He realized that the archdeacon was now about to do exactly these things, which worried him greatly, but he did not know how to refuse permission to his son-in-law.

'I'd much rather remain quiet on the matter,' he said weakly, as if apologizing.

'Quiet?' said the archdeacon, his voice echoing round the room. 'Do you wish to be quietly reduced to poverty? Nonsense, warden, we must act. Have someone ring the bell and tell the men I shall speak to them outside, in the garden.'

Mr Harding was forced to obey and the unpleasant order was given. The archdeacon stood up, fully confident of his powers of persuasion.

'I wish to be excused,' said Mr Harding, preparing not to follow him.

'For heaven's sake, don't let us show them we're divided,' replied the archdeacon. 'We must all pull together. Come, warden, don't be afraid of your duty.'

Mr Harding was afraid, afraid that he was being led to do something which was far from his duty; but he weakly got up and followed his son-in-law outside.

The old men had gathered in groups. When the two churchmen appeared, they all took off their hats, even the unwilling Abel Handy. Mr Bunce stepped forward and greeted the two gentlemen. The archdeacon then stepped forward to make his speech.

'Now, my men,' he began, 'I want to say a few words to you. Your good friend the warden here, and the bishop for whom I speak, would be very sorry if you had any reason to complain about your circumstances. Any good reason for a complaint would be removed by one of us without the need for you to send any petition to anyone.' Here he stopped for a moment, expecting some signs of grateful agreement from his audience; but no such signs came. Even Bunce sat silent, with tight lips. 'Without the need for a petition of any kind at all,' he repeated. 'But I'm told that you have already sent a petition to the bishop.'

'Yes, we have,' said Handy.

'And in it, I'm told that you say you do not receive what you think you should receive according to Hiram's will.'

'Yes, that's so,' said several voices.

'Now what is it you ask for? What is it that you haven't got already? What is it — '

'A hundred a year,' answered Greg Moody, Handy's friend.

'A hundred a year!' cried the archdeacon in amazement, stretching his arms to heaven. 'A hundred a year! Why, men, you must be mad! And you talk about John Hiram's will! When John Hiram built this hospital for poor, old, weak working men, do you think he meant to turn them into gentlemen? Do you think John Hiram intended to give a hundred a year to old men with no families, who earned in the best of their time no more than a shilling or two a day? No, men, I'll tell you what John Hiram meant. He meant that twelve old men should come here in their poverty to enjoy the care and protection offered by the Church; and here they should prepare themselves for death and make their peace with God. That was what he meant. You have not read John Hiram's will. I doubt whether those dishonest advisers of yours have read it. But I have. I know what his will was, and I tell you that that was his will and that was his intention.'

Not a sound came from the old men as they sat listening to the archdeacon. They simply stared at Dr Grantly's well-filled figure, giving no sign of the anger and disgust they must have felt.

'Now let me ask you this,' he continued. 'Do you think you live worse than John Hiram intended? Haven't you each got a room of your own, and time to enjoy yourselves? Your lives are twice as good, you have ten times more money in your pocket than you had when you were working. And yet you send us a petition asking for a hundred pounds a year! You have been badly advised, made fools of by people who are simply using you for their own purposes. You will never get a hundred pence more than what you have now. In fact it is very possible that you may get less. It is very possible that the good bishop and your warden may make changes – '

'No, no, no,' interrupted Mr Harding, who had been listening with increasing alarm and unhappiness to his son-in-law's speech. 'No, my friends, I want no changes – at least no changes that would make your lives worse.'

'May God be with you, Mr Harding,' said Bunce. 'We know you were always our friend.'

The archdeacon had not finished his speech, but he felt that he could not continue it now, so he led the way back to the house, followed by his father-in-law.

'Well,' he said, as soon as they were alone, 'I think I spoke to them plainly.'

'Yes, you were plain enough,' said the warden, without enthusiasm.

'And that's the important thing,' said Dr Grantly, clearly well pleased with himself. 'With people of this lower sort one must speak plainly or they will not understand. But they did understand, I'm sure. They knew what I meant.'

Privately, the warden thought they had understood too well.

'Now I'll just look in at Chadwick's office,' said the archdeacon, 'and then I'll go up to the palace and answer this petition of theirs.'

The warden's mind was very troubled. He had been greatly embarrassed by the archdeacon's speech but he was painfully afraid of a disagreement with any person on any subject. He thought he would give almost anything to avoid the storm which he felt sure was coming. He did not yet question the fact that he deserved his comfortable, quiet life, but he felt horror at the thought of being made the subject of common gossip and public criticism. He walked up and down his garden for hours, turning these thoughts over in his mind, feeling that he must soon make some kind of decision.

During this time the archdeacon went about his business well contented. Finding the petition in his father's library as he expected, he wrote a short answer to the men. He told them that they had no reason to complain but instead many reasons to be grateful. He made sure that the bishop signed this reply, called for his carriage and returned home to Mrs Grantly at Plumstead Episcopi.

♦

After much painful thinking Mr Harding was able to make only one firm decision: he would not show himself to be hurt over the hospital question or allow it to cause any quarrel either with Bold or with the old men themselves. Some time ago he had promised Eleanor that they would hold a little party – a musical evening – at their home and, although he did not really feel in the mood for this event, he did not wish to disappoint his daughter. When Eleanor asked him about it, she was glad to hear him say: 'I was thinking of asking Mr Bold, so I have already written him a note of invitation; but you must write one to his sister.'

Mary Bold was older than her brother, aged just over thirty. She was not beautiful or particularly clever but she had a clear sense of right and wrong and was extremely kind-hearted. People who knew her only on the surface were not greatly impressed but those who got to know her well became very fond of her, and Eleanor Harding was among the fondest of all her admirers. Eleanor had never talked openly to Mary about her brother but each understood the other's feelings about him. Brother and sister were at home together when the two invitations arrived.

'How odd that they should send two notes,' said Mary. 'I wonder why.'

Her brother understood immediately that Mr Harding's note

to him was a peace-offering, but it is always easier for the victim to be generous. John Bold felt that, as things stood, he could not go to the warden's party.

'Well, ' said Mary, 'I suppose we must both write separate letters of acceptance.'

'You'll go, of course, Mary,' said John, 'but I cannot, though I wish I could with all my heart.'

'And why not, John?' asked Mary. 'Don't tell me that you've quarrelled with Eleanor!'

'No indeed,' said her brother. 'I've no quarrel with her.'

'What is it, John?' said Mary, looking at him with a troubled, loving face.

'Well, you see, Mary,' he said at last, 'I've taken up the case of those twelve old men at Hiram's Hospital and of course that brings me into a difficult relationship with Mr Harding.' He then began to explain the whole problem to his sister.

'But why are you doing this, you who have known Mr Harding so long? Surely, John, as his friend, as a young friend – '

'Age has nothing to do with it, Mary. If an action is the right one, personal feelings must not be allowed to interfere. Of course I greatly like Mr Harding, but that is no reason for failing in my duty to those old men.'

'And Eleanor, John?' said Mary, looking at him shyly.

'Eleanor, that is, Miss Harding, if she wishes – but there is no need to talk about Eleanor Harding now. I do know that she would never blame me for doing what I know is my duty.'

Mary sat silent for some time. She wrote the first words of her reply, but then she stopped and looked at her brother.

'Oh, John, I beg you to think again about all this.'

'About what?' he said

'About the hospital and Mr Harding and the old men. Oh, John, think of Eleanor. You'll break her heart and your own too. You are going to make yourself and Eleanor and her father terribly unhappy – and for what? For a dream of turning wrong into right.'

'You don't understand, my dear girl,' said John.

'I do understand, John. I know how much you love Eleanor. At least let me say that you will go to this party. Do not break with the Hardings, if your mind is in any doubt.'

'My mind is not in doubt,' said John, after a pause. 'I could never respect myself again if I were to give in now, just because Eleanor Harding is beautiful. I do love her and I would give anything to feel sure that she loves me but I cannot for her sake step back from the work I have begun.'

So poor Mary Bold sat down and sadly finished her note, accepting for herself and making excuses for her brother.

♦

The party eventually took place as arranged. Fat old ladies chatted with fine old gentlemen, and pretty young ladies were admired by rather stiff young gentlemen, while everyone drank quantities of excellent tea and ate pieces of delicious cake. Later, lamps were brought, music desks put up and Mr Harding played his cello, joined by a young fellow-musician on the piano, to the great satisfaction of his invited audience. Then the young men began to entertain the young ladies while the older guests settled down to play cards, until it was time for everyone to express their thanks and make their way home.

Finally Mr Harding was left alone with his daughter. 'Well, Eleanor,' he said, 'are you ready for bed?'

'Yes,' she said, 'but, papa, Mr Bold was not here tonight. Do you know why?'

'Well, Eleanor, I can only guess.'

'Oh, papa, do tell me,' she cried, throwing her arms around him. 'What is going on? What is it all about? Is there any – ' she was unsure of the word to use – 'any danger?'

'Danger, my dear? What sort of danger?'

'Danger to you, danger of losing – oh, papa, why haven't you told me all this before?'

Mr Harding knew all about his daughter's love for John Bold. As a loving father he naturally thought that it was her own problems and not his that were troubling her. He looked at her in silence and then gave her a tender kiss. 'Tell me, Nelly, do you like Mr Bold very much?'

This question took Eleanor by surprise, because her feelings about John were complicated. She admitted to herself that she loved him and she knew that he admired her but she was angry that, in spite of this, he was ready to turn against her father and threaten his peaceful way of life. So when she spoke of danger, she meant danger to him, not to herself.

'So, Nelly, do you like him? That's a poor word: do you love him?'

Eleanor lay in her father's arms without answering.

'Come, my love,' her father said, 'tell me how you feel about John and I shall tell you all about my problems with the hospital.'

So Mr Harding told his daughter the whole story, taking great care to praise John Bold and not to blame him; and then, reminding her that it was late, he sent her up to her room with tearful eyes and a suffering heart.

♦

At breakfast next morning there was no further discussion of the matter. The following day John Bold met Miss Harding walking along a quiet leafy path near the cathedral, where he had hoped to find her.

'My sister tells me,' he said rather hurriedly, 'that you had a delightful party the other evening. I was so sorry I could not be there.'

'We were all sorry,' said Eleanor coolly.

'I believe, Miss Harding, you understand why at this moment – ' Bold hesitated, started again, paused but could not continue his carefully prepared speech.

Eleanor made no attempt to help him. 'Please don't apologize, Mr Bold. My father, I know, will always be glad to see you, if you visit him; his feelings towards you are quite unchanged. Where your own opinions are concerned, you are of course the best judge of those.'

'Your father is always kind and generous. But you, Miss Harding, I hope you will not think badly of me because – '

'Mr Bold,' she said, 'you may be sure of one thing: I shall always consider my father to be right and those who are against him to be wrong. If some of these people do not really know him, there can be some excuse; but those people who ought to know him well, and to love and respect him – of them I am forced to form a very different opinion. I wish you good day, Mr Bold.'

And with a cold look she stepped quickly past him, leaving her admirer in a far from comfortable mood.

Chapter 4   Uncertainty, Suffering and Doubt

Though Eleanor Harding seemed to leave John Bold with self-confidence, her heart was in a very different condition from the self-control her appearance suggested. Her father had told her repeatedly that Bold was doing nothing unfair or ungenerous, so why should she feel so cold towards him? As she walked away she would have given the world to take him by the hand, using her feminine arts to persuade him to give up his plan, and so save her father at the cost of herself; but she had been too proud to do this and had left him without one look of love or one kind word.

'But you, Miss Harding, I hope you will not think badly of me because — '

Poor Bold walked away in low spirits, his self-confidence badly shaken. He felt that he would never win back Eleanor's respect unless he could agree to give up the matter which he had promised to support. However, it would not be easy to give up, and in any case how could a girl with Eleanor's high principles learn to love a man who turned away from the path of duty?

As far as his attempts to bring changes to the hospital were concerned, Bold had good reasons to feel pleased. All Barchester was talking about the problem and every day the case was growing in size and weight. But, most important of all, the daily *Jupiter*, that all-powerful national newspaper, had mentioned it:

We have been informed of a great injustice concerning the warden of an old hospital for poor people belonging to Barchester Cathedral. The hospital gets its income from rented lands and buildings. The old people for whom the hospital exists have received no advantage from the increase in the value of the houses and land over the last four centuries, since all this increase has gone into the warden's pocket. It is simply no answer to say that twelve old men receive enough for their daily needs. By what arguments of law or tradition can the warden explain why he receives such a large income for doing nothing? Does he ever ask himself just what are the services he is being paid for? Or does the idea never enter his head? With shock and shame we must express our opinion that only in the Church of England, and only among its officials, can an example of such selfishness be found.

It is easy to imagine how troubled Mr Harding's mind was after reading this newspaper article. How was he to answer this? How could he explain to those thousands of newspaper readers that he was no robber, but a simple, modest man who had innocently accepted what was innocently offered to him?

'Write to the *Jupiter*,' said the bishop. The archdeacon did not agree. 'In such matters the *Jupiter* is all-powerful. By writing to protest, you will simply put yourself more in the wrong and become open to further attack.'

The article in the *Jupiter*, although it deeply upset the warden, was seen as an enormous success by the opposite side. Bold was sorry that the attack on Mr Harding had been so personal, but he was delighted that such a powerful independent voice had taken up his cause. Finney, his lawyer, felt enormous pleasure at being on the same side as the *Jupiter*.

The old men at the hospital had also heard about the newspaper article and were impressed that this great instrument of truth had taken up their case. Abel Handy went from room to room, repeating everything he understood was printed there (though he was unable to read it himself), with some extra ideas of his own which he felt should be added. Jonathan Crumple dreamed of soon being rich and Job Skulpit realized how right he had been to sign the petition, and said so twenty times. Even Billy Gazy became restless, and Mr Bunce kept alone, with sadness in his heart, because he guessed that evil days were coming.

Sir Abraham's opinion on the Hiram's Hospital crisis was still unknown, and the uncertainty, suffering and doubt of the people of Barchester remained extreme.

♦

Our story now moves once more to the archdeacon's bedroom at Plumstead. The lady of the house was making up her face, while the archdeacon was next door in his dressing-room.

'It's your fault,' called Mrs Grantly through the half-open door. 'I told you from the beginning how it would end, and papa has no one to thank but you.'

'Good heavens, dear,' said the clergyman from the doorway, wiping his face with a towel, 'how can you say that? I am doing my best.'

'I wish you had never done so much,' said his wife bitterly. 'If you had just let John Bold come and go at the hospital, as he and papa wanted, he and Eleanor would be married by now and we would not have heard one word more about the whole hospital business.'

'But, my dear – '

'Oh, it's all very well, archdeacon, and of course you're right: you never admit that you could be wrong. But the fact is that, by protesting so loudly, you've just made the young man more stubbornly determined.'

'But, my love – '

'And all because you didn't want John Bold as a brother-in-law. How is poor Eleanor going to find someone better? Papa hasn't got a shilling of his own and, though you can say she's pleasant-looking, she's not the sort to turn men's heads. I don't know how she can marry someone better than John Bold, or even someone half as suitable.'

Dr Grantly felt this attack was most unfair, but what could he say? A few months ago the idea of having Bold as a brother-in-law would have made him very angry. Since then, matters had changed. Bold's show of power had quite impressed the archdeacon and he was beginning to think that such a marriage would not have been a bad thing. However, he still believed firmly in 'no surrender'. He tried to encourage Mrs Grantly once more and for the twentieth time he began to tell her of the talents of Sir Abraham Haphazard.

'Oh, Sir Abraham!' she said, picking up her house keys before making her way downstairs. 'Sir Abraham won't get Eleanor a husband! Sir Abraham won't get papa another income when they've driven him out of the hospital! Listen to me, archdeacon. While you and Sir Abraham are fighting this case, papa will lose his position and what will you do then, I'd like to know, with him and Eleanor on your hands?

And anyway, who's going to pay Sir Abraham? I suppose he will not take on this case for nothing.' And with these words the good lady went downstairs to join her children and servants at family prayers, the model of a good, obedient wife.

After an excellent breakfast the archdeacon went off to that most private place, his workroom, telling the family that he was going to be very busy but that he would see Mr Chadwick if he called. When he reached his workroom he took out paper, pen and ink and laid them on his desk. Then he yawned, stretched and walked across the room to lock the door. Having made these preparations, he threw himself into a comfortable chair, opened a secret drawer beneath his table, took out a tasty French novel and began to read.

After an hour or two there was a knock at the door and Mr Chadwick's name was given. Immediately the French novel went back into the secret drawer and the comfortable chair was pushed into the shadows and, when the archdeacon unlocked the door, he was found by the manager working as usual on important Church matters. Mr Chadwick had just come from London and was known to be bringing important news.

'We've got Sir Abraham's opinion at last,' said Chadwick, passing him a copy of what the attorney-general had written. 'He has recognized a weak point in the opposite party's argument. They are directing their case against Mr Harding and myself, but Sir Abraham believes that we are only paid servants. The defendants in the case should have been either Barchester city or the Church or your father the bishop.'

'So Mr Bold is taking aim in the wrong direction, is he?' said the archdeacon.

'Haphazard thinks that any direction would be the wrong one. A lawsuit brought against the bishop might be the most dangerous, but, as Sir Abraham says, by arguing and delaying you could involve the other side in costs of fifteen thousand pounds before the matter was properly settled.'

The archdeacon clapped his hands together delightedly, thinking of the serious problems that his enemies would soon be facing.

'Don't let anyone see this document, though, archdeacon, because people will talk. We don't want the other side to find out how to fight their own battle, do we? No one in Barchester except you and me ought to see it.'

'No, no, certainly no one else,' said the archdeacon. He opened his secret drawer and carefully put Sir Abraham's opinion away, on top of the French novel.

'We must of course tell your father and Mr Harding as much of all this as will satisfy them that the matter is doing well,' said Chadwick.

'I shall meet them both tomorrow,' said Dr Grantly. 'I shall tell them all that they need to know. You can't stay to lunch, Mr Chadwick? Well, I realize your time is valuable.' And with these words the Doctor shook hands with the manager and saw him to the door.

The archdeacon was delighted. He knew that Mr Harding could never afford to pay the legal costs, which would be enormous, and that he and his father would have to pay most of them. But this did not discourage him. More important still was the victory of the Church, and this was the end to which all his energies were employed.

Chapter 5   A Council of War

The following day a meeting was arranged between Dr Grantly, his father the bishop and Mr Harding. The archdeacon arrived

The following day a meeting was arranged between Dr Grantly,
his father the bishop and Mr Harding.

first and had little difficulty in persuading his father that all was going well. On his arrival the warden took up his usual place at the bishop's elbow, affectionately asking after his old friend's health.

'Sir Abraham's opinion has come at last,' began the archdeacon.

'It is quite encouraging,' said the bishop, pressing his friend's arm. 'I'm so glad.'

'Yes,' said the archdeacon, 'Sir Abraham has paid very close attention to this case and his opinion is that the other side hasn't got a leg to stand on.'

'But how is that, archdeacon?'

'Well, under Hiram's will two paid officials have been chosen for the hospital: one to look after the men and the other to look after the money. You and Chadwick are these two servants and no one can criticize either of you for receiving a fixed wage for your work.'

'That does seem clear,' said the bishop.

'Yes, quite clear,' agreed the archdeacon. 'The amount of pay such servants receive depends on the market value of the services at any time; and those who manage the hospital should be the only judges of this.'

'And who does manage the hospital?' asked the warden.

'Oh, let them find that out; that's a quite different question. They are bringing this lawsuit against you and Chadwick, and now you have a full and perfect defence.'

'But according to that,' said Mr Harding, 'I might just as easily have sixteen hundred a year as eight, if the managers decide to give me that amount. And if I myself am one of the managers, in fact the chief manager, that can hardly be a fair arrangement.'

'Oh, that really has nothing to do with it. The main thing is to stop this young man and his cheating lawyers from interfering in an arrangement which everybody knows is fair and serviceable to the Church.'

Mr Harding sat silent for some time. At last he said, 'Did you see Sir Abraham's opinion, archdeacon?'

The archdeacon said that he had not – that is to say, he had, but he had not seen the opinion itself, he had seen what might be called a copy, whether of the whole or part of it.

'I would like to see the opinion,' said the warden, 'or at least a copy of it.'

'I suppose you can, if you insist; but I don't see the use myself. It is extremely important that no one should know its content, and so we do not wish to make extra copies.'

'Why should no one know its content?' asked the warden in puzzlement.

'What a question to ask!' cried the archdeacon, throwing up his hands in horror. 'But it is just like you – you are as innocent as a child in matters of business. Can't you see that we must do nothing to inform or help the enemy?'

'You mean that we are not to make public the fact that we have asked advice from this famous lawyer and that he has told us that Hiram's will is fully and fairly carried out?'

'Good heavens,' said the archdeacon, 'why should we say anything about Hiram's will?'

The warden now got up and began to walk nervously up and down the room. 'What about the *Jupiter*?' he asked suddenly, showing that his mind had certainly not been put at rest.

'Oh, the *Jupiter*,' answered the archdeacon. 'That can't do any real damage; you must just suffer that. In any case the matter is too unimportant to be mentioned again unless we ourselves bring it up.'

The warden continued his walking up and down. The hard, stinging words of the newspaper were fresh in his memory. 'If it can be proved,' he burst out at last, 'that I have an honest right to my income, as I have always believed I had, I am just as ready as any other person to enjoy it. I am eager to clear my name and prove to the world that I have been on the side of right. But if it cannot be proved, I will give up my position here. I cannot suffer all this pain. Could you expect me to suffer it?' he asked the bishop, almost in tears.

'No, no, dear friend,' replied the bishop tenderly, 'you must only do what your heart tells you to be right.' Unwisely he asked his son to support his point of view.

The archdeacon could not feel sympathetic, but he could advise. 'If you were to give up the wardenship just to show that you can live without it, you would be giving encouragement to rebels of every kind to make similar attacks on the Church. It would be weak. It would be wrong. It would be simply cowardly.'

'Cowardly?' cried the bishop in protest.

'Well, is it not cowardly if one cannot face the evil things one is falsely accused of? No one who really knows you will think the worse of you because of what the *Jupiter* says.'

The poor warden gave a heavy sigh and his friend the bishop echoed the sigh more gently but the archdeacon paid no attention. 'You simply cannot give up this position. You owe it to my father, who offered it to you, to those who held the wardenship in the past and to those who may hold it in the future; and you owe it to us, your brothers in the Church.' The archdeacon having finished his speech, stood observing its effects on his two listeners.

The poor warden felt unable to breathe. The archdeacon's speech had silenced him, shaken him, almost destroyed him; but it had not satisfied him. He could not see the future clearly, but he saw a battle being prepared – a battle which would take away the few comfortable things left in his life.

He sat and looked at the archdeacon, as a bird might look at a snake.

'I hope you agree with me,' said the archdeacon at last, breaking the silence. 'And, Bishop, I hope *you* agree with me too.'

'Yes, I suppose so,' said his old father slowly.

'And you, warden?'

'Do not press me for an answer just at present. I shall do nothing without careful thought, and I will give you and the bishop notice before I do it.'

Without another word he left the room. He did not breathe freely until he found himself alone outside the palace. He walked slowly, for a long time, thinking about his troubled situation, trying without success to find some weakness in the archdeacon's arguments. Then he made his way home, having decided to suffer it all, the shame and the pain, as he had been pressed to do by those whom he believed best able to advise him.

♦

Mr Harding had never been a sadder man than when he returned to his own house that day. He wandered into the sitting-room, where his daughter was, but he felt unable to speak to her and went instead to the library. He was not quick enough to escape Eleanor's sharp eyes, however. She saw that he was upset and after a few moments she followed him. She found him sitting in his chair with no book or pen or music in front of him. He was doing nothing, looking at nothing, thinking of nothing: he was simply suffering.

'Leave me, my dear, because I am busy,' he said.

Eleanor, seeing how upset he was, went back to the sitting-room. Once again she found herself shut out of her father's troubles. She no longer expected to make him happy but simply wanted to be allowed to share his problems. It was not his conversation that she wanted but his trust.

She decided to pay a visit to Mary Bold, as she now did almost every day. John Bold was up in London, busy seeing lawyers and others involved in the case. Eleanor talked to Mary Bold about her poor father while Mary listened kindly, and then Mary told Eleanor about her brother's doings, which perhaps was kinder still.

Back at the hospital the warden sat alone, with his back against the arm of his chair. He was still sitting in the same chair, in the same position, when Eleanor came back from her visit.

Their tea was as gloomy as dinner had been. When the meal was over, Eleanor put her arms round the warden's neck and said, 'Papa, won't you tell me what it is?'

'What what is, my dear?'

'This new unhappiness of yours.'

'Oh, it's not new, my dear. We all have troubles sometimes,' he said, trying to smile.

'Papa, I will not leave you till you talk to me.'

The father kissed his daughter but still said nothing; he was shy even with his own child.

'Oh, papa, do tell me what it is. If you have sad news, let us be sad together. We are all in all to each other now.'

'My child,' he answered, 'why should you also be unhappy before it is necessary? It may be that we must leave this place; but why should you be worried till that time comes?'

'Give up your position, papa,' cried Eleanor, looking boldly into his face. 'Give it up, papa.'

It was tragic to see that look of hope and carefree happiness disappear from the warden's face as the memory of the arch-deacon came back to him. If only he could give it up, what an easy way out of all his troubles that would be!

*Eleanor put her arms round the warden's neck and said, 'Papa,
won't you tell me what it is?'*

'Papa, don't think that you must stay here because of me. I can be happy with just a couple of rooms, if I see you come in and go out with a light heart.'

At these words the warden's tears fell like rain from his old eyes. When he was able to speak again, he told Eleanor all the arguments of the archdeacon, explaining how he was unable to oppose them. Eleanor for her part encouraged him to express every feeling and to open every secret in his heart to her. And finally they began to talk about John Bold, and Eleanor told how she had loved him once but could not do so now, since he had become her father's enemy. But the warden protested that Bold was no enemy of his, and spoke of happier days when their troubles would all be over. He would never allow her love for John to be changed by this quarrel. So each supported and encouraged the other, and both went to bed in a much calmer mood than they had known for some time.

Chapter 6   Eleanor's Own Petition

As Eleanor lay awake in bed that night, she was determined to free her father from his unhappy situation; she therefore formed a plan. She would go personally to John Bold and beg him to drop the legal action which he had begun, for her father's sake. Of course she could not offer herself as a reward – that would be quite improper. Though she might continue secretly to love John Bold, any question of marriage was naturally at an end.

Finally she slept and she rose with renewed hopes the following morning. She knew that John Bold was in London but was expected home soon, so she went to visit Mary, to arrange with her a plan for a meeting with her brother. However, on entering the Bolds' sitting-room she was surprised to see John's stick and coat and various bags, which showed that he had returned.

'John came back very suddenly,' said Mary. 'He has been travelling all night.'

'Then I'll come again some other time,' said Eleanor, in some confusion.

'He will be out for the next two hours,' said Mary. 'He's with that horrible Mr Finney. He came only to see him and he goes back again to London on the night train.'

Eleanor, who had not meant to have her interview with Bold that day, realized that such a meeting must be held now or never.

'Mary,' she began, 'I must see John before he goes back.'

'Of course,' said Mary, secretly rather surprised. 'I know he'll be delighted to see you.'

'I must see him now, today, and beg him to do me a special service,' went on Eleanor with great seriousness. 'But when I have done so, there can never be anything further between us.' And she began to explain her plan for saving her father.

It was clear that Mary Bold did not follow her line of thought. It seemed quite natural that Eleanor should try to speak to Bold's better feelings with reference to her father, and it seemed to Mary quite natural that John should give way, moved by such sincere tears and pretty looks. But why his good nature should not be rewarded, when the reward would help everyone and hurt no one, was a point which her practical nature could not understand, and she said so.

'But I am sure you love him, don't you?' argued Mary. 'And I am sure he loves you better than anything in the world.'

Eleanor tried to answer, but her eyes filled with tears, so she

41

walked to the window, pretending to blow her nose, and when she recovered herself she said as firmly as she could, 'Mary, this is nonsense.'

'But you do love him,' Mary insisted. 'You love him with all your heart. You cannot deny it.'

'I – ' began Eleanor, and finally burst into tears, admitting to Mary that she did love John but that it would make no difference to her decision.

While they were still talking, Bold returned and Eleanor was forced to take action. She decided to carry out her original plan and ran into her friend's bedroom to wash the marks of tears from her eyes.

'Tell him that I am here,' she said to Mary, 'and that I shall join you both soon. And remember, whatever you do, don't leave us alone together.' Eleanor then washed her face with extreme care, thinking always of her poor father; and yet she also managed to improve the arrangement of a curl or two and give some added colour to her lips, to be sure that she would make a good impression.

John Bold had not seen her since the day they had met walking near the cathedral, yet during this time he had often thought of her and considered a hundred ways of showing her how pure his love was. Sometimes when he woke in the morning he even felt like blowing his brains out but this was usually after a late-night party with Tom Towers, his friend who was a reporter for the *Jupiter*.

How beautiful Eleanor seemed to him as she walked slowly into the room. The care she had taken with her appearance was now having its effect. She had never looked more lovely to her admirer than she did now. Her face was serious but full of movement, and her full, dark eyes shone with nervous energy.

He began to talk – about London, about Barchester, about the weather, and then asked about Mr Harding's health.

'My father is not very well,' said Eleanor. 'I specially want to speak to you about my father, Mr Bold. Papa is very unhappy, very unhappy indeed, about this business of the hospital. You would pity him, Mr Bold, if you could see the suffering it has caused him.'

'Oh, Miss Harding!'

'He is a changed man. And if this goes on, he will die; he will break his heart and die. I am sure it was not you, Mr Bold, who wrote those cruel things in the newspaper.'

'Indeed it was not,' cried John Bold, who was beginning to feel extremely guilty about his friendship with Tom Towers.

'No I'm sure it was not; you would not be so cruel. But they have called my father greedy and dishonest, and they say that he is robbing the old men and taking the money of the hospital for nothing.'

'I have never said so, Miss Harding. I – '

'No,' continued Eleanor, interrupting him, the tide of her feelings carrying her on. 'No, I am sure you have not, but others have said so. And if such things are said or written again, they will kill papa! You know, I'm sure, that he is not interested in money.'

Brother and sister were both quick to agree on this point.

'It is kind of you to say so, Mary, and of you too, Mr Bold. He would leave the hospital tomorrow, and give up his house and the income and everything, if the archdeacon – ' Here she almost said 'would allow it' but instead gave a deep sigh and added, 'How I wish he would!'

'No one who knows Mr Harding personally can possibly accuse him of doing wrong,' said Bold.

'But he is the one whom you are punishing. He is the one who is suffering,' said Eleanor. 'He has never had an unkind thought in his life, never spoken an unkind word.' At this moment she burst into tears so violent that she could not speak.

For the fifth or sixth time Bold tried to say that neither he nor his friends blamed Mr Harding personally.

'Then why are you punishing him?' cried Eleanor through her tears. 'Why are you wrecking his life? Oh, Mr Bold, why did you begin all this? You whom we all so – so – valued!'

John Bold tried his best to excuse himself, with references to his public duty, and repeated how highly he valued Mr Harding's character.

By now Eleanor was again in control of herself. 'Mr Bold,' she said, 'I have come here to beg you to give up this action.'

He stood up from his seat and looked inexpressibly unhappy and uncomfortable.

'I beg you to give it up, I beg you to spare my father, to spare his life and his health, before one or the other is destroyed. I know how much I am asking and how little right I have to ask anything, but it is not for myself – it is for my father. Oh, Mr Bold, I beg you, do this for us; do not drive to desperation a man who has loved you so well.'

She did not actually kneel in front of him, but she let her soft hands rest pitifully on his arm. What pleasure this would have given him in different circumstances! But what could he say to her now? How to explain that the matter was probably beyond his control, that he could not now silence the storm which he had created?

'Surely, John, you cannot refuse her,' said his sister.

'I would give my life itself,' he said, 'if it would be of use to her.'

'Oh, Mr Bold, do not say that. I ask nothing for myself, and what I ask for my father is something which is in your power to give.'

'I would give her anything,' said Mr Bold wildly, still talking to his sister. 'Everything I have is hers if she will accept it: my house, my heart. Every hope I have is fixed on her. Her smiles are

44

sweeter to me than the sun, and when I see her sad as she is now, every nerve in my body aches. No man can love her better than I love her.'

'No, no, no,' cried Eleanor, 'there can be no talk of love between us. Will you protect my father from the evil which you have brought upon him?'

'Oh, Eleanor, I will do anything. Let me tell you how I love you.'

'No, no, no,' she almost screamed. 'This is improper of you, Mr Bold. Will you leave my father to die in peace, quietly in his quiet home? I will not leave you till you promise me.' She held on to his arm as she followed him across the room. 'Promise me, promise me,' she cried. 'Say that my father is safe. One word will do. I know how true you are; say one word and I will let you go.' Still she held him, looking eagerly into his face. Her hair was loose, her eyes were red and yet he thought he had never seen her look so lovely. 'Promise me,' she said. 'I will not leave you till you promise me.'

'I will,' he said at last. 'All I can do, I will do.'

'Then may God protect you!' said Eleanor, and began to cry like a child. Exhausted, she wanted to go now, but Bold wished to explain the situation concerning her father, and she felt the need to stay and listen to him.

Bold explained that the action against the hospital was something which he alone had started; but that now many other people had become interested in the matter, some of whom were much more powerful than himself. However, the lawyers turned to him for their instructions and, more importantly, for the payment of their bills, and he promised that he would tell them at once that he wished to give up the case. He then suggested that he would ride over to see Dr Grantly that same afternoon, to tell him of the change in his

45

intentions, and for this reason he would delay his immediate return to London.

All of this was indeed pleasant to hear, and Eleanor began to enjoy the satisfaction of feeling that she had succeeded in her purpose. She now got up to fetch her hat.

'Are you going so soon?' said Bold. 'May I not say one word for myself?'

'*I'll* fetch your hat, Eleanor,' said Mary, leaving the room.

'Mary, Mary, don't go!' cried Eleanor, but it was too late.

Now they were alone, John Bold poured out the feelings of his heart and this time Eleanor's 'no, no, no,' had no effect. She was pressed to say whether her father would be against their marriage; whether she found him acceptable; whether she preferred someone else; whether she could possibly love him; and so on. To each of these questions she was forced to give replies, so when she finally left the Bolds' home she felt that she had succeeded very well in part of her intention (to save her father) but had completely failed in the other part (to refuse any further contact with John).

Eleanor returned home not unhappy but yet not completely satisfied with herself. She felt annoyed with Mary, who had proved less dependable than expected. All she could do now, she thought, was to inform her father that John Bold was her accepted lover.

◆

John Bold got on his horse and rode off to Plumstead Episcopi, feeling rather nervous about the coming interview. From time to time he remembered the meeting with Eleanor which had just ended. On the one hand he felt the thrill of a lover who knows that he is loved; on the other hand he felt ashamed that his determination had given in so quickly to the tears of a pretty woman. How was he to face his lawyer? What was he to say to his friend Tom Towers?

On arrival he was shown into the archdeacon's workroom, with its desks and comfortable chairs. The archdeacon was standing with his back to the fireplace, ready to receive him, and his expression was one of satisfaction.

'Well, Mr Bold,' he said, 'what can I do for you? I am happy to help such an old friend of my father-in-law.'

'Please excuse my calling on you like this, Dr Grantly.'

'Certainly, certainly.'

Dr Grantly did not invite Bold to sit down, so he had to tell his story standing, with his hat in his hand. He did, however, manage to tell it, without any interruption from the archdeacon.

'And so, Mr Bold, I understand that you wish to bring this attack on Mr Harding to an end.'

'Oh, there has been no question of an attack, believe me . . .'

'Well, we won't quarrel about words. Most people would call this attempt to take away a man's income an attack, but we can call it instead a little game, if you prefer.'

'I intend to put an end to the legal action which I have begun,' said Bold stiffly.

'I understand,' said the archdeacon; 'you've already had enough of it. Well, I'm not really surprised: supporting a lost cause when there is nothing to win and everything to pay cannot be very pleasant.'

At this Bold turned very red in the face. 'You misunderstand the principles on which my actions depend, but that does not matter very much. I did not come here to discuss principles with you but to inform you of a matter of fact. Good day, Dr Grantly.'

'One moment, I have something to say in reply. You are going to end this lawsuit?'

'Yes, Dr Grantly, I am.'

'So first you allowed a gentleman who was one of your father's oldest friends to suffer all the insults which the press could throw at him; you have said publicly that it was your duty to protect those old fools in the hospital whom you have so shamefully deceived; and now you find that your game costs more than it is worth and you have decided to put an end to it. A wise decision, Mr Bold; it is just a pity that you have taken so long to reach it. Have you considered, though, that *we* may not wish to give up the case? that *we* may find it necessary to punish you for the injury you have done to us?'

Bold was now bright red with anger but he said nothing.

'We have found it necessary to employ the best advice that money can buy. You understand that these heavy costs must now come out of your own pocket. We shall not allow you to withdraw this matter from the courts.'

'You can do as you wish, Dr Grantly. Good day.'

'Let me finish, sir,' said the archdeacon. 'I have here the latest opinion from Sir Abraham Haphazard. I expect you have heard of this already, and that is the reason for your visit here today.'

'I know nothing at all of Sir Abraham Haphazard or his opinion.'

'In any case I shall tell you what it is: he considers that you do not have a leg to stand on in this matter, and that your attempts to destroy Mr Harding are completely useless. Here,' and he slapped the paper on the table in front of him. 'I have this opinion from the first lawyer in the land. Your case is in pieces, sir. And now I wish you good day, because I am busy.'

Bold had been almost speechless with anger, but now he felt so wounded and insulted that he could not leave the room without some kind of reply. 'I came here, Dr Grantly, with the warmest, kindest feelings – '

'Oh, of course you did; nobody doubts that.'

' – and you have injured me by your behaviour – '

'Of course. The damage you have done to my father-in-law must have caused you much pain.'

'The time will come, Dr Grantly, when you will understand why I called on you today.'

'No doubt, no doubt. Good day to you, Mr Bold.' And the doctor went off, closing the door behind him and making it quite impossible for John Bold to speak another word.

This was certainly the bitterest moment in John Bold's life. Not even the memory of his success in love could calm him. In fact he felt that his love for Eleanor was at the heart of the problem: it had caused him to give up the lawsuit and to be insulted; it had caused his actions to be misunderstood. This visit to the archdeacon had been a terrible mistake.

When he reached home, he rushed upstairs to the room where his sister Mary was sitting.

'If a devil really exists on earth,' he said, 'then it has the form of Dr Grantly.' He said nothing more but simply grabbed his hat, hurried out of the house and set off for London without another word.

Chapter 7   Mr Harding's Decision

The meeting between Eleanor and her father was not as stormy as the one just described but it was hardly more successful. On her return from Bold's house she found her father in a strange mood. He was walking quickly up and down the garden and she could see that he was greatly excited.

'I am going to London, my dear,' he said at once. 'I must settle this business somehow. There are some things I cannot bear.'

49

'Oh, papa, what is it?' she said, leading him by the arm into the house. 'I had such good news for you and now I'm afraid I'm too late.' Then she told him that the legal action was over and that Bold had asked her to tell her father that it would not be continued. She did not mention the new relationship she had formed with John Bold.

The warden did not seem particularly grateful for this news and, though Eleanor was not expecting to be warmly thanked, she felt hurt at the way in which her information was received.

'Mr Bold can do what he thinks proper, my love,' said Mr Harding. 'If he has done wrong, of course he will stop what he is doing, but that cannot change my purpose.'

'Oh, papa!' she cried, almost in tears, 'I thought you would be so happy – and that everything would now be all right.'

'Read that, my dear,' said the warden, giving her the latest number of the *Jupiter*, folded in such a way as to show a particular article. The topic was once again the wrongs committed by the Church. The writer heavily criticized families and individuals grown rich on income which they had not earned. It named the sons of some bishops and the grandsons of others and, having discussed these well-known personalities and their crimes, it turned finally to the subject of Mr Harding:

A few weeks ago we mentioned a case of similar injustice, though at a more modest level, in which the warden of a poor people's hospital in Barchester was receiving the greater part of the hospital's income. We refer to the question of the Barchester hospital again because we understand that a certain gentleman has taken out a lawsuit against Warden Harding on the part of the twelve old men, acting purely in the public interest. The argument for the defence is one which all fair-minded people will find completely unacceptable, namely that Mr Harding takes nothing except what he receives as a servant of the hospital, and that he

50

is not personally responsible for deciding how much he should be paid for his work. If this defence is to be offered, we hope that Mr Harding will be called as a witness to describe: the nature of his employment; the amount of work that he does; the income which he receives; and how he was given this position. We do not think he will receive much public support.

As Eleanor read this column, her face grew red with anger and, when she finished it, she was almost afraid to look at her father.

'Well, my dear,' he said, 'is it worth being a warden at that price?'

'Oh, papa, dear papa.'

'Mr Bold can't unwrite that, my dear. Mr Bold can't stop people from reading it. And what's more, my dear,' he continued, 'Mr Bold can't disprove the truth of every word you have just read – and neither can I.' Eleanor stared at him, hardly understanding what he was saying. 'I have thought deeply about all this since we were together last night,' said her father, and he came and put his arm around her waist as he had done then. 'I have thought a lot about what the archdeacon has said and what this newspaper says, and I do believe I have no right to be here.'

'No right to be warden of the hospital, papa?'

'No right to be warden with eight hundred a year, no right to such a house as this, or to spend on luxuries money that was intended for charity. Mr Bold may do as he likes about his lawsuit but I hope he will not give it up for my sake.'

Poor Eleanor! Believing till now that she had done so much, she suddenly felt that her attempts had resulted in nothing; it was not a pleasant feeling.

'They must not put forward this argument in my defence,' continued the warden. 'The man who wrote the article is right

51

when he says that such a defence is disgusting to an honest mind. I will go up to London, my dear, and see these lawyers myself; and if no better excuse can be made for me than that, I must leave the hospital.'

'But the archdeacon, papa?'

'It can't be avoided, my dear. There are some things which a man cannot bear; I cannot bear that.' And he put his hand on the newspaper.

'But will the archdeacon go with you?'

'No, I think not,' he said. 'I think I shall start before the archdeacon is ready. I shall go early tomorrow morning.'

'That will be best, papa,' said Eleanor, understanding very well her father's way of thinking.

'The fact is, my dear, I wish to do all this before the archdeacon can – can interfere. He will accuse me of being weak and cowardly, but I know that I ought not to remain here. So, Nelly, we shall have to leave this pretty place.'

Eleanor's face grew bright as she told her father how completely she agreed with him. She could see that he was once more his usual happy self.

'We shall live at Crabtree Parva. That also has a very pretty garden.' Crabtree Parva was a church where Mr Harding had been a clergyman in the past and which was now looked after by a younger colleague, a married man with half a dozen children. The house at Crabtree was very modest, as the income was – only eighty pounds a year.

Eleanor told her father that she herself would have no regrets about leaving the house or giving up the horses; she was simply happy that he would escape from all the troubles which surrounded him at present.

'But we will take the music, my dear.'

And so they went on planning their future happiness. Finally the warden did thank Eleanor for what she had done and

Eleanor did find an opportunity to tell him her secret. Her father showed that he was delighted and said that the man she loved was honest, true and kind-hearted – 'a man to whom I can trust my dear child with safety'.

Eleanor ran upstairs to prepare her father's clothes for the journey, and the warden returned to his garden to say goodbye to every tree and plant that he knew so well.

◆

Still suffering from the archdeacon's insults and deeply annoyed with himself, Bold returned to London. His interview with the archdeacon had gone badly wrong, but he still felt it necessary to keep his promise to Eleanor and he set off to do this with a heavy heart.

The lawyers whom he had employed in London received his instructions with surprise and considerable doubt but they were forced to obey, expressing their regret that the heavy costs would fall on their own employer when it would not have been difficult to throw them on the opposite side.

He next thought of the newspapers. The leader of the attack was of course the *Jupiter*. He knew Tom Towers very well and had often discussed with him the matter of the hospital. Bold could not say whether the pieces which had appeared in the newspaper were written by his friend; Towers was always very cautious in such matters and unwilling to talk about the newspaper's plans. However, Bold believed he had written the words which had caused such pain in Barchester and he felt it was his duty to prevent him from repeating them. This idea led him from the lawyers' office to the place which formed the centre of Tom Towers's operations.

Tom Towers lived comfortably in an apartment in the Temple.★

★ The Temple is a part of London where lawyers have their offices.

The room in which he usually worked was filled with books and works of art. He was enjoying a final cup of tea, surrounded by a sea of newspapers, when his servant brought in John Bold's visiting-card. Tom Towers told the boy to show his friend in. The two men were about the same age and had known each other since Tom was a poor law student, struggling to earn a living as a newspaper reporter. Tom Towers was now more powerful than most politicians, though few people knew his name. Some people believed that Tom Towers was the most powerful man in Europe, with the appearance of an ordinary person but the powers of a god.

Chapter 8   Persuading the Press

'Ah, Bold! How are you?' cried his friend.

'And how are you? I suppose you're busy?' inquired Bold.

'Yes, but if I have a free hour in the day, this is it.'

'I want to ask you if you can help me in a certain matter.'

Towers understood from his friend's voice that he was referring to the newspaper. He smiled but made no promise.

'You know the lawsuit I've been busy with?' said Bold. 'Well, I've given it up.'

Tom Towers simply lifted one eyebrow and waited for his friend to continue.

'Yes, I've given it up. The fact is that the behaviour of Mr Harding – Mr Harding is the – '

'Oh yes, you mean the warden – the man who takes all the money and does nothing,' said Tom Towers, interrupting him.

'Well, I'm not sure about that. But he has behaved so extremely well in this matter, so unselfishly, so openly, that I cannot continue with the case and so cause him harm.' Bold's heart remembered Eleanor as he said this, but he felt that what he said was not untrue.

'It's the old story of the traditional rights of the person holding the position,' said Towers. 'But what happens if that person holds a traditional wrong, and the traditional rights lie with the poor people, if only they knew how to get at them? Isn't this case something like that?'

Bold could not deny it but thought that it was one of those cases which needed careful management before any real good could be done.

'It will cost you a fair amount, I'm afraid,' said Towers.

'A few hundred pounds – perhaps three hundred,' said Bold. 'I can't help that and I'm prepared for it.'

'That's philosophical! It's quite unusual to hear a man talking of his hundreds in such an unemotional manner. But I am sorry that you are giving up the case; it damages your good name if you start something like this and don't bring it to a finish.'

'I couldn't continue it,' said John Bold, 'because I found I was in the wrong.'

Tom Towers seemed rather unconcerned. 'In that case,' he said, 'of course you must give it up.'

'And I have called this morning to ask you also to give it up,' said Bold, trying to hide his embarrassment.

'To ask me?' said Tom Towers, with the most gentle smile and a look of innocent surprise.

'Yes,' said Bold, showing great hesitation. 'The *Jupiter*, you know, has taken the case up very strongly. Mr Harding has felt its criticisms deeply. I thought if I could explain to you that he personally has not been to blame, these newspaper articles might be discontinued.'

Tom Towers's face was a model of calmness as this suggestion was made. He showed no sign either of agreement or disagreement. 'My dear friend,' he said, when Bold had finished speaking, 'I really am not responsible for what the *Jupiter* does.'

'Come on, Towers,' said Bold, taking courage as he remembered his promise to Eleanor, 'I have no doubt in my own mind that you wrote the articles yourself, and they were very well written. All I am asking is that in future, for my sake, you will make no personal reference to Mr Harding.'

'My dear Bold,' said Tom Towers, 'I have known you for many years and value your friendship. I hope you will let me explain to you that none of us connected with the press can properly allow any kind of interference.'

'Interference!' cried Bold. 'I don't want to interfere.'

'Indeed you do, my friend. What else do you call it? You think that I am able to keep certain remarks out of a newspaper. Your information is probably incorrect but you think I have such power and you are asking me to use it; that is called interference. Now, if I had this power, as you believe, and was ready to use it as you want me to, would that not be very improper? It is the independence of great newspapers like the *Jupiter* which has earned them so much respect in the eyes of the public. Think about this carefully and you'll see that I am right.'

Bold realized that it was useless to argue further. He said goodbye and left the room as quickly as he could, in his own mind accusing his friend of obvious dishonesty. 'I know he wrote those articles,' said Bold to himself, 'and I know he got his information from me. He was quite willing to believe my word absolutely when it suited his own opinions but when I offer him information which offends his views, he tells me that private considerations are damaging to the high principles of the press! What is any public question but a collection of private interests? What is any newspaper article but the expression of the views held by one side?' It was the completely unshakeable position

*'My dear friend, I really am not responsible for what
the* Jupiter *does.'*

which his friend held on what was right and wrong that made Bold so angry, and this same quality which made such a position secretly so attractive.

♦

The good warden had to use his modest ability to deceive to get out of Barchester without being stopped on the way. The evening before he had written a note to the archdeacon, explaining his intentions of making this journey and, if possible, of seeing the attorney-general. He excused himself for not informing Dr Grantly earlier, saying that his decision had been a very sudden one. He then gave the note to Eleanor, on the understanding that it would be sent over, but not too quickly, to Plumstead Episcopi.

The warden had also prepared a note for Sir Abraham Haphazard, explaining who he was and begging the great gentleman to spare him a ten-minute interview at any time on the following day. Mr Harding knew that the archdeacon would follow him to London as soon as he received his note but he judged that for this one day he was safe. If he could manage to see Sir Abraham that day, he would have carried out his purpose before the archdeacon could interfere.

On arriving in London the warden drove to the hotel near St Paul's★ where he had stayed in the past. He ordered dinner and then set off to visit the attorney-general in his office. There he was told that Sir Abraham was in court. Mr Harding left his note. He asked to have an answer that same evening and said he would return to receive it. When he returned he was given his own note back again, with this message written in pencil on it: 'Tomorrow, 10.00 p.m., my office. A.H.' 10.00 p.m.! What an hour to choose for a legal interview!

★ The famous cathedral church in London.

The next day he had breakfast at nine and told the waiter, 'If anyone calls for me, I am going to eat out and I shall return about eleven o'clock this evening.'

We shall not describe the nervous wanderings in which the poor warden spent the next twelve hours until the time of his appointment, though they seemed endless. A clock was striking ten as he knocked on Sir Abraham's door, where a clerk informed him that the great man would be with him immediately.

Chapter 9   The Law Gives its Opinion

Mr Harding was shown into a comfortable library and was not kept waiting long. After ten or fifteen minutes the attorney-general entered.

'Very sorry to keep you waiting, Mr Warden,' said Sir Abraham, shaking hands with him, 'and sorry too about the lateness of the hour, but it was the best I could do.'

Sir Abraham was a tall, thin man whose hair was grey but who did not look old in other ways. His hard face gave him the appearance of a machine with a mind, full of intelligence but empty of natural feelings. He was as bright and sharp and cold as a diamond. He knew everyone whom it was useful to know and yet he had no friends. The one thing which he respected was success and he knew of no one as successful as himself.

'And so, Mr Warden,' said Sir Abraham, 'all our troubles with this lawsuit are at an end. You need trouble yourself no further about it. Of course they must pay the costs, so the cost to you and Dr Grantly will be very small.'

'I'm afraid I don't quite understand you, Sir Abraham.'

'Don't you know that their lawyers have advised us that they have withdrawn the lawsuit?'

Mr Harding explained that he knew nothing of this, though

59

he had heard of some such intention. Finally he also succeeded in making Sir Abraham understand that even this did not satisfy him; and he began to explain his point of view.

'I know I have no right to trouble you personally with this matter, but as it is of the greatest importance to me, as all my happiness is concerned with it, I thought I might dare ask your advice. The truth is, Sir Abraham, that I am not fully satisfied with this matter as it stands at present. I can clearly see that the finances of the hospital are not arranged according to the will of John Hiram.'

'No such organizations are, Mr Harding, nor can they be. The changed circumstances in which we live make it impossible.'

'That is quite true, but I can't see how those changed circumstances give me the right to eight hundred a year. I don't know whether I have ever read John Hiram's will but if I read it now, I would not understand it. What I want you to tell me, Sir Abraham, is this: do I as warden have a legal right to what remains of the income after the twelve old men have been fully taken care of?'

Sir Abraham said that he couldn't exactly say it in so many words that Mr Harding had a legal right, etc, etc, etc, and ended by expressing his strong opinion that it would be madness to ask any further questions on the matter as the lawsuit was going to be – in fact already was – withdrawn.

Mr Harding, sitting in his chair, began to play an imaginary cello. 'I can resign,' said Mr Harding, slowly playing away with one hand.

'What! Give up your position completely?' said the attorney-general, looking at him in total amazement.

'Did you see those articles in the *Jupiter*?' said Mr Harding, almost sure that Sir Abraham would be sympathetic to the embarrassment he had felt.

Sir Abraham said that he had seen them. The idea that this poor little clergyman could be forced to resign because of a newspaper article was so insane that he hardly knew how to talk to him as a sensible human being.

'Wouldn't it be better to wait,' he said, 'until Dr Grantly comes to town? Wouldn't it be better to delay your decision until you are able to get his advice?'

Mr Harding said firmly that he could not wait and Sir Abraham began seriously to doubt that he was sane. 'Of course,' he said, 'if you have a private income large enough to cover your needs and if this – '

'I haven't a sixpence of my own, Sir Abraham,' said the warden.

'Good heavens! Then Mr Harding, how do you intend to live?'

Mr Harding explained that he would continue to receive eighty pounds a year for his work as precentor and that he had a right to the clergyman's place at Crabtree, which would bring him another eighty pounds. He mentioned that these two positions involved duties which might be difficult to carry out at the same time but that there was the possibility of changing places with a colleague.

Sir Abraham listened in pitying amazement. 'I really think, Mr Harding, that you should wait for the archdeacon. This is a very serious step – one which, in my opinion, you have absolutely no need to take. A man is never the best judge of his own situation.'

'A man is the best judge of what he himself feels. I would rather be poor for the rest of my life than read another article like the two which have appeared, feeling, as I do, that the writer has truth on his side.'

'Don't you have a daughter, Mr Harding – an unmarried daughter?'

'I have, Sir Abraham, and she and I are in complete agreement on this subject.'

'Excuse me for saying so, Mr Harding, but shouldn't you be more conscious of your daughter's happiness? For her sake, give up this idea.'

'But if this income is not lawfully mine, then she and I will both have to beg,' said the warden, in a voice much sharper than before.

'My dear sir, nobody questions its lawfulness.'

'Yes, Sir Abraham, one person does question it – I question it myself. It may seem strange to you, Sir Abraham, that I lived for ten years without giving any thought to these matters until they were made violently known to me by a public newspaper. But now my sense of right and wrong is fully awake, I must obey it. When I came here today I did not know that Mr Bold had withdrawn his lawsuit, and my purpose was to ask you to give up my defence. As there is now no action, there can be no defence. I would like you to know that, from tomorrow, I shall no longer be warden of the hospital.' And as he finished speaking he played a complicated tune with wild movements of his arms.

Sir Abraham looked at him with great surprise: a few minutes ago so shy and hesitant and now so full of strong, even violent feelings. 'You'll sleep on this, Mr Harding, and tomorrow – '

'I have done more than sleep on it.' said the warden. 'I have lain awake on it, night after night. I could not sleep on it then but I hope to do so now.'

The attorney-general had no answer to make to this, so Mr Harding finally withdrew, thanking the great man for his kind attention.

Mr Harding felt a certain amount of satisfaction as he left Sir Abraham's office. He knew that the attorney-general thought he was a fool, but he did not care. He now had to face the

'Yes, Sir Abraham, one person does question it — I question it myself.'

archdeacon, so he walked slowly back to his hotel. He rang the bell softly, his heart beating. He almost thought of escaping round the corner and delaying the storm a little longer, but he heard the slow steps of the old waiter approaching to unlock the door.

'Dr Grantly is here,' he was told, 'and Mrs Grantly. They are in the sitting-room upstairs, waiting for you.'

The warden tried to appear unconcerned as he replied, 'Oh, indeed! I'll go upstairs at once,' but he failed completely.

As the warden entered the sitting-room, the archdeacon was standing in the middle of the room with a deeply sad expression, while his patient wife sat on a sofa behind him.

'Papa, I thought you were never coming back,' said the lady. 'It's twelve o'clock.'

'Yes, my dear,' said the warden. 'The attorney-general could not see me until ten. It is late, but what could I do?' He gave his daughter a kiss, shook hands with his son-in-law and again tried to look unconcerned.

'And you have been with the attorney-general?' asked the archdeacon.

Mr Harding said that he had.

'But, papa, what did you say to Sir Abraham?' asked his daughter.

'I asked him, my dear, to explain John Hiram's will to me. He couldn't explain it in the only way that would have satisfied me, and so I resigned the wardenship.'

'Resigned it! Good heavens!' and the good archdeacon sank back in horror into an armchair. 'I'm sure Sir Abraham must have advised you to ask for guidance from your friends.'

Mr Harding said that this was correct.

'Then your threatening to resign amounts to nothing and we are just where we were before.'

Mr Harding was now moving uncomfortably from one foot to the other. In fact he did not have the least doubt in his mind about resignation, though he did have doubts about his ability to defend his decision against his son-in-law.

The archdeacon was marching up and down the room, signalling by certain shakings of his head the complete stupidity of his father-in-law. 'Why,' he said at last, 'why did you leave Barchester so suddenly? Why didn't you tell us what you were planning to do?'

The warden hung his head and made no reply. 'I think I'll go to bed,' he said at last.

'At least you'll promise me to take no further step without discussing the matter first,' said the archdeacon.

Mr Harding gave no answer but slowly lit his lamp.

'Come, warden,' said the archdeacon, 'promise Susan to give up this idea of resigning the wardenship.'

The warden looked at his daughter and said, 'I'm sure Susan will not ask me to break my word or do what I know to be wrong.'

'Papa,' she said, 'it would be madness to give up your position. What are you going to live on?'

'God who feeds the wild birds will take care of me also,' said Mr Harding with a smile. 'And I shall have my place at Crabtree,' he added.

'Eighty pounds a year!' cried the archdeacon.

'And the position of precentor,' said his father-in-law.

'My dear warden,' said Dr Grantly, 'this is all nonsense. Whether you have eighty pounds or one hundred and sixty, you still can't live on it. You can't destroy Eleanor's future like that. You simply can't resign: the bishop will not accept it. The whole thing is settled. What we must prevent now is any more newspaper articles.'

'But I shall resign,' said the warden, very, very softly.

'Then, Mr Harding, there is nothing but disaster in front of you,' said the archdeacon, unable to contain himself any longer. 'How do you mean to pay for the enormous expenses of this action?'

'I will sell my furniture,' said the warden.

'Furniture!' cried the archdeacon, marching up and down the room. 'Your father is like a child,' he said to his wife. 'Eight hundred pounds a year, with nothing to do! And he throws it away because some journalist writes an article in a newspaper! Well, I have done my duty. If he chooses to destroy his child, it is not my fault.'

There was a pause for about a minute and then the warden picked up his lamp and quietly said, 'Good night.'

'Good night, papa,' said Mrs Grantly.

As Mr Harding closed the door he heard the familiar remark – slower, heavier and gloomier than ever – 'Good heavens!'

Chapter 10   The Warden Resigns

The three met again the next morning at breakfast, a gloomy event. The archdeacon ate his toast in silence, turning over bitter thoughts in his mind. The warden tried to talk to his daughter and she tried to answer him but they both failed.

'I think I shall go back home at three o'clock today,' the warden said.

'I must go to Cox and Cummins,' said the archdeacon. 'I must once more beg you to take no further steps till you see my father. At least you owe him that much.' And without waiting for a reply Dr Grantly set off. Shortly afterwards Susan also left the room.

The warden now wrote his letter of resignation, which went like this:

My Lord Bishop,

It is with the greatest pain that I feel it necessary to resign into your hands the wardenship of the hospital at Barchester, to which you so kindly appointed me nearly twelve years ago.

I need not explain the circumstances which have made this step necessary to me. You know that a question has been asked about the right of the warden to the income which goes with the wardenship. It seems to me that this right is not built on very solid ground, and I hesitate to run the risk of accepting an income which is legally doubtful.

The position of precentor of the cathedral is, as you know, traditionally joined to that of the warden. However, unless you disagree with such an arrangement, I would like to continue the work of the precentor.

You will realize that my resignation of the wardenship does not prevent the position from being offered to someone else. I do not wish to suggest that there is harm in another person filling it or that such a person will not command my greatest respect.

I cannot finish this official letter without again thanking you for all your great kindness, and I beg to sign myself

Your most obedient servant,
Septimus Harding,
Warden and Precentor

He then wrote the following private note:

My dear Bishop

I cannot send you this official letter, which may perhaps be made public, without sending you also a warmer expression of thanks for all your kindness to me. You will, I know, understand the feelings and perhaps pity the weakness that make me resign my position at the hospital. I am not a person whose character is strong enough

67

to stand firm against public attack. If I were sure that I was absolutely in the right, I should consider it my duty to defend my position under any circumstances; but I do not have this complete certainty and I cannot believe that you will think me wrong in what I am doing.

My dear friend, let me have a line from you to say that you do not blame me for what I am doing and that the clergyman of Crabtree Parva will be the same friend to you as the warden of the hospital.

I thank you from my heart for the appointment which I am now giving up and for all your kindness; and am, dear bishop, now as always,

Yours most sincerely,
Septimus Harding

Having written these letters, Mr Harding, no longer the warden, realized that it was nearly two o'clock and that he must prepare for his journey. He packed his bag and paid his bill. He was then driven to the station with a warm glow of success in his heart. Indeed, had he not for the first time in his life held his ground against his much-feared son-in-law and against the archdeacon's wife also? Was not this a great victory?

Eleanor was waiting at Barchester station when the train came in to the platform.

'Dear papa,' she said, as soon as he told her the news, 'I'm so glad.'

♦

The morning after Mr Harding's return home, he received a note from the bishop. 'Please come and see me at once,' wrote the bishop, 'so that we may see what can be done.'

Mr Harding did go to see the bishop and there were long discussions between the two old friends. The bishop's first suggestion was that they should live together at the palace. He told Mr Harding that he needed another helper, a companion with whom to discuss Church matters. It was difficult for Mr Harding to make his friend understand that this arrangement would not suit him: he could not resign from his present appointment and then become a regular guest at the bishop's table. Mr Harding, though deeply grateful, refused this offer. His wish was to support himself, not to be supported by the charity of others.

The bishop considered that Mr Harding could continue to hold the position of precentor, an opinion with which everyone agreed.

Mr Harding allowed himself no rest until everything was prepared for his departure from the hospital. The lawyers' bill, which the archdeacon had used to frighten his father-in-law, was not as great as he had feared and was paid by the bishop, on the instructions of the archdeacon. For the present Mr Harding rented rooms in Barchester, and his music, books and instruments were taken there, together with his own armchair and Eleanor's favourite sofa. Eleanor had prepared a little bedroom for herself in one of the rooms above the chemist's shop where she and her father were going to stay.

The day for the move was fixed and all Barchester was greatly excited. Opinion was divided about the correctness of Mr Harding's action. The businessmen, the officers of the town and most of the ladies were loud in his praise; he was gentlemanly, generous, upright. But the professional people, especially the lawyers and clergymen, had a different way of thinking. They said that Mr Harding had shown weakness, an absence of fellow-feeling. His resignation would do much harm and very little good.

On the evening before he left he asked all the old men to his sitting-room to say goodbye. The wine and glasses were on the table and the chairs arranged round the room. The sound of old feet could be heard approaching.

'Come in, my friends, come in,' said the warden. 'Come and sit down.' And he took Abel Handy by the hand and led the old rebel to a chair.

The others followed slowly – some hardly able to walk, some almost blind. Now their old faces were covered with shame, and every kind word from their master simply increased their guilty feelings. When the news had first reached them that Mr Harding was going to leave the hospital, it was seen as a kind of victory. He had admitted that he had no right to the money about which they had petitioned, and, as it did not belong to him, it must of course belong to them. The one hundred a year owed to each of them was actually becoming a reality. Abel Handy was a hero and Bunce a false companion who had taken the enemy's side. But other rumours soon made their way into the old men's rooms. First they were told that the income given up by Mr Harding would not come to them, and the lawyer Finney told them that this was true. They were then told that Mr Harding's place would be immediately filled by someone else. They knew that a new warden could not be kinder than Mr Harding and imagined that he would be much less friendly. And then came the bitter news that from the moment of Mr Harding's departure his own special gift of twopence a day would no longer be given out. So this was to be the end of their great struggle, of their fight for their rights, of their petition, their arguments and their hopes! They were to change the best of masters for a possible bad one and to lose twopence a day each man!

'Sit down, sit down, my friends,' said the warden. 'I want to say a word to you and to drink your healths before I say goodbye. My dear old friends,' he said, 'you all know that I am going to leave you. There has been some misunderstanding between us recently. You have thought, I believe, that you did not get all that you deserved and that the income from the hospital has not been properly shared out. I myself am unable to say how this money should be divided or managed, and so I have thought it best to go.'

'We never wanted you to leave us, sir,' said Handy.

'No indeed, sir,' said Skulpit, 'we never thought it would end like this.'

'No,' went on Mr Harding, 'I am sure you did not wish to turn me out, but I thought it best to resign. And now that I am about to leave you, I dare to offer you my advice.'

The men all said that such advice would be most welcome.

'Another gentleman will probably take my place here very soon, and I strongly advise you to receive him in a friendly manner and not to discuss among yourselves the amount of his income. You are well looked after here and I do not think that your position can be improved.'

'It's true, sir, what you say. We see it all now,' cried one of the old men.

'Yes, Mr Harding,' said Bunce, speaking for the first time. 'I believe they do understand it now, now that they have driven from under their roof the best warden that they will ever know – and just when they stand in most need of a friend.'

'Come, come, Bunce,' said Mr Harding, blowing his nose and wiping his eyes.

'Oh, none of us ever wanted to do Mr Harding any harm,' said Handy. 'If he's leaving now, it's not because of us. And I don't see why Mr Bunce speaks against us like that.'

'You've spoiled your lives and you've spoiled mine too, and that's why,' said Bunce.

'Nonsense, Bunce,' said Mr Harding, 'nobody's life is spoiled. I hope that we shall all leave as friends, that you'll all drink a glass of wine in a friendly spirit with me and with one another. You'll have a good friend too in your new warden, I'm sure. And remember that I'm not going so far away that I shall not be able to come and see you sometimes.'

Mr Harding filled all the glasses, and himself gave one to each man. Then, lifting his own, he said, 'I hope you may all live contented, trusting in God and thankful for the good things he has given you.'

These poor old men felt guilty and ashamed to have driven the good warden from his happy home to spend his old age in some strange place. They did their best, however; they drank the wine and left. Mr Harding shook hands and spoke a kind word to each one as he departed. Finally only Bunce remained.

Mr Harding went sadly back to his sitting-room and Bunce went with him. The good warden did what he could to make his old friend happier but poor old Bunce felt that his days of happiness were gone. 'My life is over,' he said. 'I have now to forgive those who have injured me – and then die.'

And so the old man departed and Mr Harding himself finally burst into tears.

Chapter 11 Happiness

The following morning Mr Harding walked out of the hospital arm in arm with his daughter and quietly entered his new apartment in town. There was a tear in Eleanor's eye as she left, but Mr Harding walked with a firm step and a look of satisfaction on his face.

It was not long before the archdeacon brought up the subject of a new warden with his father. Naturally he expected to be asked to recommend someone, and he had three or four suitable clergymen on his list. He was greatly amazed when his father decided that no one would be appointed in Mr Harding's place. 'If we can put matters right, Mr Harding will return,' he said, 'and if we cannot, it would be wrong to put any other gentleman into so cruel a position.' It was useless for the archdeacon to argue, to insist and even to threaten; nothing could persuade his father to fill the vacant place.

The hospital itself has suffered over the years since Mr Harding left it. No one now lives in the warden's house. Six of the old men have died and their places remain unfilled. Quarrels divide the six who are left. The hospital building has been kept in good condition by Mr Chadwick, who still acts as manager, but the whole place has become untidy and ugly. The warden's garden is uncared-for and wild, the flower beds empty and the grass uncut. A few years ago it was the prettiest place in Barchester and now it is a matter of shame to the city.

♦

Mr Harding did not go to Crabtree Parva in the end. Instead, he was put in charge of a tiny church within the walls of the city. It is no bigger than an ordinary room, but it is still a perfect church. Here he holds the afternoon service every Sunday, and always in the front row is to be seen the faithful Mr Bunce. Mr Harding is still the precentor in the cathedral. He leads a contented life. He still lives in the rooms he rented when he left the hospital, but now he has them to himself. Three months after the move Eleanor became Mrs Bold and of course went off to live with her husband.

The marriage itself created some difficulties. The archdeacon, whose feelings were still strong, could not agree to be present at the event himself, although he allowed his wife and children to go. The marriage took place at the palace and the bishop himself took the service. About six months after the wedding, the archdeacon agreed to meet John Bold at a dinner party and since that time they have become almost friends. The archdeacon firmly believes that marriage has opened John Bold's eyes to the great truths of religion, and Bold has come to think that time has softened the rougher parts of the archdeacon's character.

Mr Harding, then, is a happy man. His time is spent mainly at his daughter's or at the palace. He is never left alone for long, and within a year of Eleanor's marriage his determination to live alone had changed enough for him to allow his cello to be kept ready for him at his daughter's house.

Every other day a message is brought to him from the bishop. 'The bishop is not very well today and he hopes Mr Harding will dine with him.' In fact, although the bishop is over eighty, he is never ill. Mr Harding does dine with him very often, which means going to the palace at three and remaining there till ten; and if he does not go, the bishop is in a complaining mood and goes off to bed an hour before his usual time.

It took a long time for the people of Barchester to stop calling Mr Harding 'Mr Warden'. Today if someone calls him by that name, he always says with a smile, 'Not warden now, only precentor.'

ACTIVITIES

Chapters 1–5

Before you read

1 Look at the pictures in this book. How long ago does the story take place? How can you tell?

2 These words all come in this part of the story. Use a dictionary to check their meaning.

article   carriage   cello   charity
lawsuit   petition   warden   will

Now match each word with one of the meanings below:

a a musical instrument with strings
b written instructions about what to do with your property after you die
c a formal request
d a vehicle pulled by horses
e a piece of writing in a newspaper or magazine
f an organization created for the good of others
g a legal action in the courts
h the head of a school or college

After you read

3 Can you identify these people?

a energetic, confident, a good speaker, decisive
b brave, enthusiastic, amusing, young, active
c fair-minded, generous, not hard-working, musical
d not beautiful, kind-hearted, with a clear sense of right and wrong
e pleasant-looking, seemingly self-confident, very fond of her father, in love

4 Answer these questions:

a Who are the petitioners and what do they want?
b What actions does Dr Grantly take over the petition?
c In Chapter 4, what upsets Mr Harding's peace of mind?
d Why does he feel better at the end of Chapter 5?

Chapters 6–11

Before you read

5 Is Mr Harding being fair or weak over the question of his job and salary? What would *you* do in his situation? Discuss this with other students.

6 Dr Grantly says: 'We shall not allow you to withdraw the matter.' *Withdraw* means:
   a to remove
   b to delay
   c to discuss

7 Mr Harding says: 'I can resign.' *Resign* means:
   a to sign another document
   b to give up my position
   c to deny the previous statement

After you read

8 Who says these things? Who to?
   a 'But he is the one you are punishing.'
   b 'It's quite unusual to hear a man talking of his hundreds in such an unemotional manner.'
   c 'God who feeds the wild birds will take care of me also.'

Writing

9 Explain the terms of John Hiram's will concerning the hospital.

10 Imagine that you live in Barchester. You read the article in the Jupiter given on page 28. Write a letter to the newspaper, defending Mr Harding and the church's position.

11 Trollope makes some indirect criticisms of the church, the law and the press in his novel. Describe some of them.